KOREAN SHORT STORIES FOR BEGINNERS AND INTERMEDIATE LEARNERS

Engaging Short Stories to Learn
Korean and Build Your Vocabulary

1st Edition

LANGUAGE GURU

ISBN: 978-1-950321-24-7

TABLE OF CONTENTS

INTRODUCTION

We all know that immersion is the tried and true way to learn a foreign language. After all, it's how we got so good at our first language. The problem is that it's extremely difficult to recreate the same circumstances when we learn our second language. We come to rely so much on our native language for everything, and it's hard to make enough time to learn the second one.

We aren't surrounded by the foreign language in our home countries. More often than not, our families can't speak this new language we want to learn. And many of us have stressful jobs or classes to attend regularly. Immersion can seem like an impossibility.

What we can do, however, is gradually work our way up to immersion no matter where we are in the world. And the way we can do this is through extensive reading and listening. If you have ever taken a foreign language class, chances are you are familiar with intensive reading and listening. In intensive reading and listening, a small amount of text or a short audio recording is broken down line by line, and every new word is looked up in the dictionary.

Extensive reading and listening, on the other hand, is quite the opposite. You read a large number of pages or listen to hours and hours of the foreign language without worrying about understanding everything. You look up as few words as possible and try to get through material from start to finish as quickly as you can. If you ask the most successful language learners, it's not intensive reading and listening but extensive that delivers the best results. Volume is much more important than total comprehension and memorization.

In order to be able to read like this comfortably, you must practice reading in the foreign language for hours every single day. It takes a massive volume of text before your brain stops intensively reading and shifts into extensive reading.

This book hopes to provide a few short stories in Korean you can use to practice extensive reading. These stories were written for both beginner and intermediate students in mind, so they should be a little easier to digest compared to native Korean. While it's no substitute for the benefits of reading native Korean, we hope these stories help build confidence in your reading comprehension skills overall. They offer supplementary reading practice with a heavy focus on teaching vocabulary words.

Vocabulary is the number one barrier to entry to extensive reading. Without an active vocabulary base of 10,000 words or more, you'll be stuck constantly looking up words in the dictionary, which will be sure to slow down your reading. To speed up the rate at which you read, building and maintaining a vast vocabulary range is absolutely vital. This is why it's so important to invest as much time as possible into immersing yourself in native Korean every single day. This includes both reading and listening.

We hope you enjoy the book and find it useful in growing your Korean vocabulary and bringing you a few steps closer to extensive reading and fluency!

HOW TO USE THIS BOOK

T simulate extensive reading better, we recommend keeping things simple and using the short stories in the following manner. Read through each story just once and no more. Whenever you encounter a word you don't know, try to guess its meaning using the surrounding context. If its meaning is still unclear, check the vocabulary list at the end of the story. Alternatively, you could even start each story by taking a quick glance at the vocabulary list to familiarize yourself with any new words.

After completing the reading for each chapter, test your knowledge of the story by answering the comprehension questions. Check your answers using the answer key located at the end of the book.

Memorization of any kind is completely unnecessary. Attempting to push new information into your brain forcibly only serves to eat up your time and make it that much more frustrating when you can't recall it in the future. The actual language acquisition process occurs subconsciously, and any effort to memorize new vocabulary and grammar structures only stores this information in your short-term memory.

If you wish to review new information that you have learned from the short stories, there are several options that would be wiser. Spaced Repetition Systems (SRS) allow you to cut down on your review time by setting specific intervals in which you are tested on information in order to promote long-term memory storage. Anki and the Goldlist Method are two popular SRS choices that give you the ability to review whatever information you'd like from whatever material you'd like.

It's also recommended to read each story silently. While reading aloud can be somewhat beneficial for pronunciation and intonation, it's a practice aligned more with intensive reading. It will further slow down your reading pace and make it considerably more difficult for you to get into extensive reading. If you want to work on pronunciation and intonation, take the time to do it during SRS review time. Alternatively, you could also speak to a tutor in the foreign language to practice what you learned.

Trying to actively review everything you learn through these short stories will slow you down on your overall path to fluency. While there may be an assortment of things you want to practice and review, the best way to go about internalizing new vocabulary and grammar is to forget it! If it's that important, it will come up through more reading and listening to more Korean. Save the SRS and other review techniques for only a small selected sample of sentences you feel are the most important. Languages are more effectively acquired when we allow ourselves to read and listen to them naturally.

And with that, it is time to get started with our main character Byung-hoon and the eight stories about his life. Good luck, reader!

제 1 장

음식

병훈은 4주간 다이어트를 해서 벌써 5킬로그램을 뺐습니다. 새 식단이 무척 타이트하지만 최대한 비슷하게 따라하고 있습니다.

아침식사로는 된장찌개와 밥, 김치, 그리고 단무지를 먹습니다. 출근 전 시간이 많지 않지만 하루를 건강하게 보내기 위해서는 아침식사를 찌개로 시작해야 합니다. 병훈은 찌개에 두부, 양파, 마늘, 감자, 애호박, 그리고 청고추를 넣는걸 좋아합니다. 아침식사에 커피가 빠질 수 없겠죠?

점심식사로는 가벼운 식사를 통해 체중 감량을 최대화 하기 위해, 병훈은 주로 상추겉절이만 먹습니다. 파, 참기름, 참깨, 간장, 그리고 식초를 넣습니다. 적은 양의 식사이지만 많은 양을 먹어 허기를 채우고 동시에 칼로리는 적게 유지할 수 있습니다. 샐러드를 먹어도 배가 고플 땐 국도 함께 먹습니다. 주로 칼로리가 낮은 콩나물국을 선택합니다.

저녁식사로는 그 날 무엇을 원하느냐에 따라 몇 가지 옵션이 존재합니다. 당면과 시금치, 당근, 그리고 버섯을 볶아 만드는 한국 전통 음식인 잡채를 먹을 수도 있고, 나물과 밥 그리고 고추장을 섞어 건강에 좋은 비빔밥을 먹을 수도 있습니다. 여름이기 때문에 국물에 단백질이 풍부한 콩국수를 먹을 수도 있습니다. 어떤 것을 선택하더라도 요리를 해야겠지만 전부 그럴만한 가치가 있습니다.

다섯번째 주가 시작될 때까지 병훈의 다이어트는 잘 지속되고 있었습니다. 많은 사람들이 그렇듯, 그는 스트레스를 많이 받는 힘든 일을 하기 때문에 매번 끼니를 준비할 시간이 있지는 않았습니다. 에너지는 떨어지기 시작했고 식욕과 배고픔은 급격히 증가하기 시작했습니다.

곧, 아침식사는 된장찌개에서 달콤한 시리얼 한 그릇으로 변해버렸고, 블랙으로 마시던 커피는 이제 우유와 설탕으로 가득하게 되었습니다.

항상 회의에 늦어서, 점심식사로 먹던 샐러드는 패스트푸드로 바뀌었습니다. 원래 점심식사때는 물을 마셨지만 이젠 청량음료를 마십니다.

시간이 흐른 후의 저녁식사는 절망적일 뿐이었습니다. 병훈은 일 때문에 지쳐서 돌아와 요리를 할 수가 없었습니다. 피자, 아이스크림, 감자튀김, 그리고 감자칩이 훨씬 쉬운 선택이었고 그의 불안감에서 관심을 돌리는데에 도움을 주었습니다.

몇 주가 흐른 후, 그는 감량했던 5킬로그램은 원래대로 되돌아왔고, 심지어 원래 몸무게 보다 5킬로그램이 더 쪘습니다! 이 실패로 인해 병훈은 더욱 기분이 나빠졌습니다. 다음 다이어트때는 더욱 더 엄격한 식단을 선택하고 음식을 덜 먹겠다고 맹세했습니다.

안타깝게도, 이렇게 엄청난 칼로리 하락으로 인해 그만큼 에너지 수치가 하락하고 불량 식품에 대한 갈망이 커진다는 것을 깨닫지 못하고 있습니다. 식단 조절을 할때 건강한 음식을 먹으면서 칼로리 섭취를 서서히 줄이는 것이 훨씬 더 현명한 방법을 깨닫기 까지는 많은 시도가 필요할 것 같습니다.

단어 목록

- 음식 — food

- 킬로그램 — kilos (kilograms)

- 살을 빼다 — to lose weight

- 식단 — diet

- 타이트하다 — to be tight, to be strict

- 최대한 — the maximum

- 아침식사 — breakfast

- 된장찌개 — doenjang-jjigae (soybean paste stew)

- 밥 — steamed rice

- 김치 — kimchi

- 단무지 — pickled radish

- 출근하다 — to go to work

- 찌개 — stew

- 두부 — tofu

- 양파 — onions

- 마늘 — garlic

- 감자 — potatoes

- 애호박 — Korean zucchini

- 청고추 — green chili peppers

- 커피 — coffee

- 점심식사 — lunch
- 가벼운 식사 — light meal
- 체중 감량 — weight loss
- 선호하다 — to prefer
- 주로 — mainly
- 상추겉절이 — Korean lettuce salad
- 파 — green onions
- 참기름 — sesame oil
- 참깨 — sesame seeds
- 간장 — soy sauce
- 식초 — vinegar
- 많은 양 — large portions
- 채우다 — to fill up
- 칼로리 — calories
- 유지하다 — to maintain
- 국 — soup
- 콩나물국 — kongnamulguk (soybean sprout soup)
- 저녁식사 — dinner
- 옵션 — options
- 존재하다 — to exist
- 당면 — cellophane (sweet potato) noodles

- 시금치 — spinach

- 당근 — carrots

- 버섯 — mushrooms

- 볶다 — to stir-fry

- 한국 전통 음식 — classic Korean dish

- 잡채 — japchae (Korean glass noodle stir-fry)

- 나물 — seasoned vegetables

- 고추장 — gochujang (Korean hot pepper paste)

- 섞다 — to mix

- 건강에 좋은 — healthy

- 비빔밥 — bibimbap (Korean mixed rice dish)

- 여름 — summer

- 국물 — broth

- 단백질 — protein

- 콩국수 — kongguksu (soy milk noodle soup)

- 요리 — cooking

- 가치 — worth

- 지속하다 — to keep up, to continue

- 스트레스를 많이 받는 힘든 일 — stressful and demanding job

- 끼니를 준비하다 — to prepare a meal

- 만큼 — as much as

- 에너지 — energy
- 떨어지다 — to decrease
- 식욕 — appetite
- 배고픔 — hunger
- 급격히 증가하다 — to rise rapidly
- 달콤한 시리얼 — sweet cereal
- 그릇 — bowl
- 우유 — milk
- 설탕 — sugar
- ~으로 가득하게 되다 — to be full of
- 회의 — meetings
- 패스트 푸드 — fast food
- 물 — water
- 청량음료 — soda, soft drinks
- 시간이 흐르다 — time goes by
- 절망적 — hopeless
- 지치다 — to be exhausted
- 피자 — pizza
- 아이스크림 — ice cream
- 감자튀김 — french fries
- 감자칩 — potato chips

- 불안감 — anxiety
- 관심을 돌리다 — to take one's mind off something
- 원래대 — original
- 되돌아오다 — to regain
- 심지어 — even, what was worse
- 몸무게 — weight
- 살이 찌다 — to gain weight
- 실패 — failure
- 맹세하다 — to vow
- 안타깝게도 — unfortunately
- 엄청나다 — to be huge
- 거대한 하락 — massive reduction
- 깨닫다 — to realize
- 수치 — level
- 불량 식품 — junk food
- 갈망 — cravings
- 조절하다 — to control, to adjust
- 섭취 — intake
- 서서히 줄이다 — to slowly reduce
- 현명하다 — to be wise
- 시도 — attempts

이해력 문제

1. 샐러드를 먹어도 배가 고플 때, 병훈은 점심으로 무엇을 더 먹을까요?
   A) 샌드위치
   B) 생선
   C) 국
   D) 아무것도 먹지 않는다

2. 병훈이 제일 좋아하는 저녁식사는 무엇인가요?
   A) 잡채
   B) 비빔밥
   C) 콩국수
   D) 이야기에 병훈이 제일 좋아하는 저녁식사가 언급되지 않습니다.

3. 병훈의 다이어트의 다섯번째 주에 무슨일이 일어나기 시작했나요?
   A) 에너지 수치가 증가하고, 식욕과 배고픔은 급격히 하락하기 시작했습니다.
   B) 에너지 수치가 하락하고, 식욕과 배고픔은 급격히 증가하기 시작했습니다.
   C) 에너지 수치는 그대로 였고, 식욕과 배고픔은 급격히 증가하기 시작했습니다.
   D) 에너지 수치가 하락하고, 식욕과 배고픔은 그대로 였습니다.

4. 피자, 아이스크림, 감자튀김, 그리고 간식거리는 주로
   무엇으로 여겨지나요?
   A) 건강한 음식
   B) 균형잡힌 아침식사
   C) 불량 식품
   D) 저칼로리 식품

5. 병훈이 다이어트를 시작할때 90 킬로그램 이었다면,
   이야기가 끝날 때 병훈의 몸무게는 몇이었을까요?
   A) 85 킬로그램
   B) 90 킬로그램
   C) 95 킬로그램
   D) 100 킬로그램

English Translation

Byung-hoon has been on a diet now for four weeks and has already lost five kilos. His new diet is very strict, but he follows it extremely closely.

For breakfast, he eats doenjang-jjigae with some steamed rice, kimchi, and pickled radish. There's not much time before he has to go to work, but starting his day with stew is important for him in order to eat healthy throughout the day. In his stew, he likes to put tofu, onions, garlic, potatoes, Korean zucchini, and green chili peppers. As for his drink, what breakfast would be complete without a cup of coffee?

For lunch, Byung-hoon prefers to eat a light meal to maximize his weight loss, so he usually has just Korean lettuce salad. In his salad, he puts green onions, sesame oil, sesame seeds, soy sauce, and vinegar. It may be a small meal, but he can eat large portions to help satisfy his hunger while keeping the calories low. If the salad does not fill him up, he'll also eat some soup. Usually, it's soybean sprout soup, as it's also very low in calories.

For dinner, there are a few options available, depending on what he wants that night. He can have japchae, a classic Korean dish made up of stir-fried sweet potato noodles mixed together with spinach, carrots, and mushrooms. Or he can have bibimbap, which is another healthy choice because of the variety of seasoned vegetables combined with rice and gochujang. And since it's the summer, he can also have kongguksu, which is high in protein because of the soy milk broth. All choices require some cooking, but it's worth it in the end.

All was going pretty well for Byung-hoon until the fifth week started. Like many of us, he works a stressful and demanding job, so there wasn't always enough time to prepare every meal. His energy started dropping, while his appetite and hunger started rising rapidly.

Soon, the doenjang-jjigae for breakfast became the large bowl of sugary cereal. And the black coffee was now drowned in milk and lots of sugar.

The salad for lunch turned into fast food meals, since Byung-hoon was always running late for meetings. Originally, he was drinking water with this meal as well as every meal, but now it was soda.

And dinner was just hopeless after a while. Byung-hoon would come home exhausted from work and could not bring himself to cook. Pizza, ice cream, French fries, and potato chips were much easier choices and helped take his mind off all the anxiety.

Several weeks later, he had regained all five kilos he had lost and even gained an additional five kilos on top of that! The failure made Byung-hoon feel even worse. He vowed, for his next diet, that he would be even more strict and eat even less food.

Unfortunately, he doesn't realize that the massive drop in calories is causing an equally massive dip in his energy levels and cravings for junk food. It would take many attempts before he finally learned that starting his diet with lots of healthy foods and slowly cutting down calories would be the wiser move.

제 2 장

운동

___

병훈은 운동을 통해 자기 관리를 더 잘해야 겠다고 마음 먹었습니다. 스트레스도 풀고 찐 살을 빼는데도 도움을 줄 것입니다. 다음주부터 일주일에 다섯번 씩 달리는 조깅을 시작할 것 입니다.

첫째 날에는, 출근 전 한참 일찍 일어나 테니스화를 신고 시작하기만을 기다립니다. 약간의 기본적인 스트레칭 후 조깅이 시작되고 모든 것이 잘 풀리고 있는 것 같습니다. 하지만 2분 뒤 병훈은 벌써 숨이 찹니다. 그는 헉헉대고 있고 그의 숨은 점점 가빠집니다. 그리고 5분 뒤, 조깅은 걷기운동으로 바뀝니다. 병훈은 몸이 정상이 아니라는 것을 깨닫게 됩니다.

시간이 지나고, 몇 일은 몇 주가 되고 몇 주는 몇 달이 됩니다. 병훈은 이제 쉬지 않고 30분을 달릴 수 있습니다. 1~2년 내로 마라톤을 뛸 수도 있겠다고 그는 생각합니다. 자신의 발전이 자랑스럽지만, 심폐지구력 발달 외에 아무것도 하지 않는 건 이제 지겨워졌기 때문에 다음 단계로 방식을 변경을 하기로 합니다.

병훈의 친구들인 민준과 주원이 퇴근 후 웨이트 트레이닝을 같이 하자고 병훈을 초대해 헬스장에서 다같이 모여 함께 시간을 보내려 합니다. 일주일에 다섯번씩 운동 프로그램에 전념하기로 결정합니다. 매 주 가슴, 등, 어깨, 다리, 그리고 팔 같은 하나의 신체 부위를 정해서 운동하기로 합니다.

하루하루가 고되지만, 운동후의 엔도르핀 분비는 모든 노력을 가치있게 만듭니다. 몸을 식히기 위해 남자들은 런닝머신 위에서 걷거나 사우나에서 10분간 땀을 흘리며 긴장을 풉니다.

시간이 흐르고, 병훈은 웨이트 트레이닝이 자신과 맞지 않는다고 결정 내립니다. 민준과 주원은 너무 경쟁심이 강하고, 운동은 재미보다 고통에 가까워졌습니다. 헬스장에서 요가 교실이 진행되기 때문에 병훈은 기대를 하며 요가에 등록합니다.

수업들은 몸의 긴장을 풀고 정신을 안정 시킬 수 있도록 고안된 다양한 스트레칭과 포즈들을 가르칩니다. 쉽지 않은 수업이라 모든 수강생들이 땀을 뻘뻘 흘립니다. 하지만 웨이트 트레이닝에 비하면 강도가 덜 하고 조깅에 비해 훨씬 재밌고 편안합니다. 병훈은 매 수업마다 상쾌한 기분으로 다음에 또 오기를 기약하며 떠납니다. 그는 심지어 몇몇 아름다운 수강생들과 대화도 하고 매 주 다시 보기를 기다리게 됩니다. 이렇게 추가적인 보너스도 있는 운동 입니다.

단어 목록

- 운동 — exercise
- 자기 관리 — self-management
- 마음 먹다 — to make up one's mind
- 스트레스 — stress
- 조깅 — jogging
- 한참 일찍 — very early
- 테니스화 — tennis shoes
- 약간의 — some
- 기본 스트레칭 — basic stretches
- 잘 풀리다 — to go well, to work out well
- 숨이 차다 — to be out of breath
- 헉헉대다 — to become short of breath
- 점점 — gradually
- 숨이 가빠지다 — to become hard to breathe
- 몸이 정상이 아니다 — to be out of shape
- 마라톤을 뛰다 — to run a marathon
- 발전 — progress
- 자랑스럽다 — to be proud
- 심폐지구력 — cardio
- 발달 — development

- 단계 — step, stage
- 방식 — way, means, method
- 퇴근 — get off work, come home from work
- 웨이트 트레이닝을 하다 — to lift weights
- 초대하다 — to invite
- 헬스장 — gym
- 모이다 — to gather
- 시간을 보내다 — to spend time
- 운동 프로그램 — workout program
- 전념하다 — to commit, to devote
- 신체 부위 — body part
- 가슴 — chest
- 등 — back
- 어깨 — shoulders
- 다리 — legs
- 팔 — arms
- 고되다 — to be hard, to be tough
- 엔도르핀 분비 — endorphin rush
- 몸을 식히다 — to cool down
- 런닝머신 — treadmills
- 사우나 — sauna

- 땀을 (뻘뻘) 흘리다 — to sweat (profusely)
- 긴장을 풀다 — to relax
- 경쟁심이 강하다 — to be competitive
- 고통 — pain
- 요가 교실 — yoga classes
- 진행하다 — to proceed
- 등록하다 — to register, to sign up
- 수업들 — lessons
- 몸의 긴장을 풀다 — to loosen the body
- 정신을 안정시키다 — to calm the mind
- 고안되다 — to be designed (to /for)
- 다양한 — various
- 스트레칭과 포즈 — stretches and poses
- 수강생들 — students, trainees
- 비하다 — to compare
- 강도 — intensity
- 편안 — comfortable
- 상쾌한 기분 — refreshing feeling
- 기약하다 — to promise
- 몇몇 — some
- 추가적 보너스 — extra incentive

이해력 문제

1. 병훈은 어떤 종류의 신발을 신고 뛰었나요?
   A) 운동화
   B) 테니스화
   C) 하이힐
   D) 러닝 부츠

2. 병훈은 왜 조깅하는 것을 멈췄을까요?
   A) 목표를 달성해서
   B) 일찍 일어나는게 피곤해서
   C) 너무 지겨워서
   D) 마라톤을 뛰기 싫어서

3. 병훈, 민준, 그리고 주원은 무엇에 집중하는 운동 프로그램
   에 전념 했나요?
   A) 가슴, 등, 어깨, 다리, 그리고 팔.
   B) 가슴, 등, 달리기, 다리, 그리고 심폐지구력.
   C) 가슴, 수영, 어깨, 달리기, 그리고 팔.
   D) 요가, 심폐지구력, 조깅, 웨이트 트레이닝, 그리고
      스포츠.

4. 이 글의 남자들은 운동 후 어떻게 몸을 식히나요?
   A) 음악을 들으며 런닝머신에서 뛰기
   B) 간단한 10 분 요가 루틴을 하기
   C) 수영장에서 수영을 하거나 뜨거운 샤워를 하기
   D) 런닝머신에서 걷거나 사우나에서 10 분간 땀 흘리기

5. 병훈은 왜 웨이트 트레이닝을 그만 두었나요?
    A) 너무 심심해서
    B) 운동의 강도가 너무 심하고 경쟁적이여서
    C) 민준과 주원이 먼저 그만 두어서
    D) 부상을 당해서

English Translation

Byung-hoon decides that he should really start taking better care of himself by exercising. It will help manage his stress and even help him lose the extra weight he put on. Starting next week, he will begin a jogging routine, where he will run five days a week.

On the first day, he wakes up extra early before work and puts on his tennis shoes, eager to get started. After some basic stretches, the jogging starts, and everything seems to go well. Within two minutes, however, Byung-hoon is out of breath. He's wheezing, and his breathing becomes super heavy. And after just five minutes, the jogging is replaced by walking. He realizes the truth. He is out of shape.

As time passes, days become weeks. Weeks become months. Byung-hoon is now able to run continually for 30 minutes. Within a year or two, he could be running a marathon, he thinks. While he's proud of his improvement, doing nothing but cardio has grown extremely boring, so a change of routine is the next step.

Byung-hoon's friends Min-jun and Joo-won have invited him to come lift weights after work, so they all meet at the gym, eager to spend some time together. They decide to commit to a workout program five days a week, where they will work one body part per week: chest, back, shoulders, legs, and arms.

Each day requires strenuous effort, but the endorphin rush at the end of each workout makes it all worth it. To cool down, the men relax by walking on the treadmills or sweating it out in the sauna for 10 minutes.

Some time passes, and Byung-hoon decides that weightlifting isn't a good fit for him. Min-jun and Joo-won get too competitive with it, and the intensity of the workouts has become more painful than fun. At the gym, however, they offer yoga classes, so Byung-hoon signs up, eager to start.

The classes teach a variety of stretches and poses designed to loosen the body and calm the mind. The lessons are not easy by any means, and they make all the students sweat. Yet, it's not as intense as weightlifting. And it's much more fun and relaxing than jogging. Byung-hoon leaves each class feeling refreshed and excited to come back for more. He even starts chatting with some pretty girls whom he looks forward to seeing every week. It's a routine with an extra incentive to maintain.

제 3 장

취미생활

"같이 수강하는 여자들 중 한명과 데이트 할 수 있으면 정말 좋겠다" 라고 병훈은 생각했다. "저들 중 한명과 공통점을 찾으면 관계를 만들어 나갈 수도 있을거야."

그의 취미생활은 대중에게 관련이 있는 것들이 많았습니다. 병훈을 포함한 누구나 티비와 영화를 보는것을 좋아하지만, 게임을 좋아하는 여자를 찾을 수 있을까요? 만약 찾지 못한다면, 자기만큼 프로야구와 농구에 빠져있는 사람을 찾을 수 있을까요? 정치, 역사, 그리고 정부에 대해 대화할 사람이 있다면 정말 좋을텐데요.

요가교실에서 처음으로 만난 여자는 민서였습니다. 그녀의 첫인상은 아주 똑똑해 보였습니다. 책을 많이 읽는 사람이었는데 비소설보단 소설을 좋아했습니다. 그녀는 문학에 굉장히 열정적이고 현재 읽고 있는 소설에 대해 몇 시간이고 말할 수 있었습니다. 그외에도 그녀는 자신의 개를 돌보고 산책을 시키는데 많은 시간을 들였습니다. 가끔은 와인 한 병을 즐기며 공포영화를 보곤 했습니다.

두번째로 알게 된 여자는 서연이였습니다. 항상 가야할 곳이 있었던 바쁜 그녀는 대화할 시간이 많지 않았습니다. 그녀가 아주 건강하고 몸매가 좋은 것은 누구나 다 아는 사실이었고 병훈은 나중에 그녀가 여성 보디빌딩 선수이자 코치인 것을 알게 되었습니다. 혹시나 고객과의 약속이 없는 날에는 사업을 하느라 항상 바빴습니다. 서연은 SNS 스타였고, 티셔츠, 스웨터, 모자, 액세서리 등을 판매하는 의류 브랜드 또한 만들었습니다. 그녀를 일 중독자라고 할 수도 있겠지만 그녀가 매우 성공적인 사람임은 틀림없었습니다.

병훈이 마지막으로 시간을 보내게 된 여성은 사교성이 아주 뛰어난 하윤이였습니다. 그녀가 다니는 모임에는 말하고 함께 놀 친구가 많았고 그녀가 외향인임이 아주 분명했습니다. 문자를 하고 있지 않으면 밖에서 친구들과 놀고 있거나, 술을 마시거나, 클럽에 가있었죠. 혹시라도 집에 있기로 결심한 날에는 일본 애니메이션을 보거나 게임을 하고 놀았습니다.

병훈은 하윤에게 곧바로 끌리기 시작했습니다. 최신 게임과 발매예정 게임에 대해 얘기할 수 있는 상대를 드디어 찾았기 때문이죠. 하지만 이 둘의 성격은 잘 어울리지 못했습니다. 궁합이 전혀 맞지 않았습니다. 공통적인 취미생활 외에는 결코 다른 할 이야기가 없어 보였습니다.

서연은 대화할 시간이 별로 없었지만 민서는 병훈과 함께 시간을 보낼 의향이 있었습니다. 병훈은 그녀가 가장 좋아하는 책에 대해 말하는 것을 듣고 심지어 그녀의 설득으로 오디오북을 통해 책을 읽기도 했습니다. 민서는 스포츠나 역사에 관심이 많지는 않았지만 병훈이 자신이 관심있는 주제에 대해 이야기 할때 보이는 열정과 에너지에 끌렸습니다. 서로에 대한 이런 관심은 그들이 사귀기 시작하기에 충분한 이유가 되었습니다.

단어 목록

- 취미생활 — hobbies

- 데이트를 하다 — to go on a date

- 공통점을 찾다 — to find something in common

- 관계를 만들다 — to make a connection

- 관련이 있는 — relatable

- 포함하다 — to include

- 티비와 영화를 보다 — to watch TV and movies

- 게임 — video game

- 프로 야구 — professional baseball

- 농구 — basketball

- 정치 — politics

- 역사 — history

- 정부 — government

- 첫인상 — first impression

- 똑똑하다 — to be smart

- 비소설 — non-fiction

- 소설 — fiction

- 문학 — literature

- 열정적 — passionate

- 개를 돌보다 — to take care of a dog

- 산책하다 — to take a walk

- 시간이 들다 — to take time

- 와인 한 병 — bottle of wine

- 즐기다 — to treat oneself

- 공포영화를 보다 — to watch horror movies

- 알게 되다 — to get to know

- 몸매가 좋다 — to be in great shape

- 여성 보디빌딩 선수 — female bodybuilding athlete

- 코치 — coach

- 혹시나 — by any chance

- 고객 — client

- 사업을 하다 — to manage a business

- 약속 — appointment

- SNS 스타 — social media star

- 티셔츠 — T-shirts

- 스웨터 — sweat shirts

- 모자 — hats

- 액세서리 — accessories

- 판매하다 — to sell

- 의류 브랜드 — clothing brand

- 일 중독자 — workaholic

- 성공적인 — successful
- 사교성 — sociability
- 뛰어나다 — to be excellent, to be outstanding
- 함께 놀다 — to hang out
- 외향인 — extrovert
- 분명하다 — to be clear
- 문자를 하다 — to text
- 클럽에 가다 — to go clubbing
- 집에 있다 — to stay home
- 결심하다 — to decide
- 일본 애니메이션 — Japanese anime
- 곧바로 — immediately
- 끌리다 — to be attracted to
- 최신 — the newest
- 발매예정 — upcoming
- 상대 — someone, partner
- 성격 — personalities
- 궁합 — romantic chemistry
- 전혀 — none at all
- 공통적인 — mutual
- 의향이 있다 — to be willing to do

- 설득 — persuasion
- 오디오북 — audiobooks
- 스포츠 — sports
- 관심 — interest
- 주제 — topic, subject
- 서로 — mutual
- 사귀다 — to date, to go out (with)
- 충분하다 — to be enough

이해력 문제

1. 다른 사람과 공통점이 있다는건 무엇을 뜻할까요?
   A) 서로를 좋아한다
   B) 서로를 사랑한다
   C) 서로를 좋아하지 않는다
   D) 둘 다 관심있는 공통된 취미가 있다

2. 정치, 역사, 그리고 정부는 보통 무엇으로 분류되나요?
   A) 소설
   B) 비소설
   C) 문학
   D) 전부 해당 됨

3. 서연은 여성 보디빌딩 선수일 뿐만 아니라 또 무엇이었나요?
   A) 개인 사업가
   B) 알코올 중독자
   C) 요가 강사
   D) 매우 사회적인 사람

4. 외향인을 가장 잘 표현한 보기는 무엇인가요?
   A) 시끄럽고 짜증스러운 사람
   B) 용감하고 대담한 사람
   C) 말을 잘하고 사교적인 사람
   D) 수줍음을 잘 타고 조용한 사람

5. 이 이야기에서 가장 궁합이 잘 맞았던 커플은 누구인가요?
   A) 병훈과 하윤
   B) 병훈과 서연
   C) 병훈과 민서
   D) 병훈과 요가강사

English Translation

"It would be really nice to go on a date with one of those girls from class," Byung-hoon thinks to himself. "Hopefully, I can find something in common with one of them and maybe make a connection."

His hobbies were somewhat relatable. Everybody likes watching TV and movies, including Byung-hoon, but would he be able to find a girl who likes video games? If not, could he find someone into professional baseball and basketball as much as he was? It would be amazing if he had someone to talk to about politics, history, and government.

The first girl he met from yoga class was Min-seo, who seemed really smart right away. She was a big reader, but of fiction rather than non-fiction. Her passion was literature, and she could talk for hours about the current story she was reading. Besides that, she spent a lot of time taking care of her dog and taking him for long walks. And occasionally, she'd treat herself to a bottle of wine and watch horror movies.

Seo-yeon was the second girl he got to know from class, although she didn't always have a lot of time to talk. There was always somewhere she needed to be. It was obvious that she was extremely fit and in great shape, and Byung-hoon later learned that she was a female bodybuilding athlete and coach. If she didn't have an appointment with a client, she was busy building her business. Seo-yeon had a big social media following and built a clothing brand that sold T-shirts, sweat shirts, hats, and accessories. You could say she was a workaholic, but you had to admit she was very successful.

The last girl Byung-hoon spent time with was Ha-yoon, who was a bit of a social butterfly. She had a large social circle of friends to talk to and hang out with. It was clear that she was an extrovert.

If she wasn't texting, she was out with friends, drinking and clubbing. On the occasion that she did decide to stay home, Ha-yoon would watch Japanese anime and play video games.

Byung-hoon was immediately drawn to Ha-yoon, as he finally found someone he could nerd out with about current and upcoming games. Their personalities, however, didn't seem to match very well. The chemistry just wasn't there. They never seemed to be able to talk about anything outside of their mutual hobby.

Seo-yeon never really had much time to talk, but Min-seo was more than willing to spend some time with him. Byung-hoon listened to her talk about all her favorite books, and she even convinced him to try reading a book via audiobooks. Min-seo didn't show much interest in sports or history, but she was attracted to the passion and energy Byung-hoon emitted whenever he spoke about subjects he cared about. Their mutual interest in one another was enough for them to start dating.

제 4 장

직장

병훈의 사회생활은 꽃피고 있었지만 직장생활은 정반대였습니다. 그는 보험회사 사무실에서 일하는데, 비록 급여는 좋지만 업무량이 감당이 안 될 정도로 많습니다.

그가 매일 아침 업무 이메일을 확인하면 즉시 처리해야하는 요청이 50개 이상 쌓여있습니다. 점심식사 시간 전에 서둘러 이메일을 발송하고 처리하지 않으면 스케줄이 예정보다 늦어져서 초과 근무를 할 가능성이 커집니다. 이는 병훈에게 많은 스트레스를 줍니다. 특히 상사가 그의 어깨너머로 감시하고 있을 땐 더욱 더 더욱 더 많은 스트레스를 줍니다.

병훈의 상사는 모든 직원에게 엄격해야 합니다. 단 한 번의 실수만으로도 회사가 큰 손해를 볼 수 있습니다. 이런 일이 생기면 직원들 뿐 아니라 상사도 크게 징계를 받게 됩니다.

보험업계는 일하기 힘든 직종이라 약한 사람들에게는 적합하지 않습니다. 회의, 문서, 그리고 규정은 모두 아주 중요한 사항이며 그 어떤 것도 놓치거나 잊어버리면 안됩니다. 잘못하면 해고될 수도 있습니다!

"정년퇴임을 할때 까지 어떻게 버틸 수 있을까?" 병훈은 자기자신에게 적어도 일주일에 한번은 묻습니다. 이 질문이 일주일에 한번만 나온다면 다행입니다. 스트레스와 불안감이 그를 한계로 몰아가고 있습니다. 이대로는 그가 무너지기까진 시간 문제 입니다.

만약 그가 다른 대학 학위를 선택했다면 인생이 어떻게 달라졌을까요? 만약 컴퓨터공학을 골랐다면? 프로그래밍을 더

즐겼을까요? 만약 대학 야구팀에서 더욱 노력했더라면? 프로 수준까지 올라갔을까요? 고등학교때 프로게이머가 되어 비디오 게임을 생업으로 삼을 수 있었다면? 꿈이 이루어진 것과 같았을 거에요.

안타깝게도 병훈의 삶은 그렇게 되지 못했습니다. 현재 자신이 싫어하는 직업에 얽매여 있을지라도 그는 상황이 바뀔 거라는 희망을 가지고 있습니다. 그의 많은 직장동료들은 이러한 희망 조차도 없어보입니다. 그의 직장에서 우울증과 불안장애는 흔한 일이지만 분위기를 가볍게 하기 위해 즐겁게 대화하고 농담을 할 수 있는 몇몇의 동료들 또한 존재합니다. 그들 덕분에 하루를 극복하기가 조금 쉬워집니다. 그것이 가장 큰 차이를 만듭니다.

하지만 삶의 가혹함에 완전히 짓눌려 예전 자신의 껍데기에 불과해 보이는 사람들도 있습니다. 이런 사람들이 그 어느 상사보다 더 병훈을 더 겁나게 만듭니다.

그런데 상황을 언제쯤 바뀔까요? 어떻게 바뀔까요? 확실한 것은 무언가가 변해야 한다는 것 뿐입니다.

단어 목록

- 직장 — work
- 사회 생활 — social life
- 꽃피다 — to bloom
- 정반대 — polar opposite
- 보험 회사 — insurance company
- 사무실 — office
- 급여 — pay
- 업무량 — workload
- 감당이 안되는 — overwhelming
- 업무 이메일 — work email
- 확인하다 — to check
- 즉시 — immediately
- 처리하다 — to deal with
- 요청 — requests
- 쌓이다 — to pile up
- 서둘러 — in a hurry
- 발송하다 — to dispatch
- 예정보다 늦어지다 — to get caught behind
- 초과 근무를 하다 — to work overtime
- 가능성 — possibility

- 상사 — boss

- 너머 — over

- 감시하다 — to watch, to monitor

- 직원 — employee

- 실수 — mistake

- 큰 손해 — a big loss

- 징계를 받다 — to be disciplined harshly

- 직종 — occupation

- 적합하다 — to be suitable, to fit

- 문서 — documents

- 규정 — regulations

- 사항 — a matter, a subject

- 놓치다 — to miss

- 잊어버리다 — to forget

- 해고되다 — to be fired

- 정년 퇴임하다 — to retire

- 버티다 — to endure, to withstand

- 다행 — relief, lucky

- 한계로 몰아가다 — to be pushed to one's limits

- 이대로 — like this

- 무너지다 — to collapse

- 시간문제 — matter of time
- 대학 학위 — college degree
- 컴퓨터 공학 — computer science
- 프로그래밍 — programming
- 대학 야구 팀 — college baseball team
- 프로 수준 — professional level
- 고등학교 — high school
- 프로게이머 — pro-gamer
- 생업으로 삼다 — to do for a living
- 꿈이 이루어지다 — to have a dream come true
- 얽매다 — to tie up, to bind
- 희망 — hope
- 직장동료 — colleague
- 조차도 — even, so much as
- 직장 — workplace
- 우울증 — depression
- 불안장애 — anxiety disorder
- 흔하다 — to be common
- 분위기를 가볍게 하다 — to lighten the mood
- 농담을 하다 — to crack jokes
- 동료 — colleagues

- 존재하다 — to exist

- 덕분에 — thanks to

- 하루를 극복하다 — to get through each day

- 큰 차이를 만들다 — to make all the difference

- 가혹함 — harshness

- 짓눌리다 — to be crushed

- 예전 자신의 껍데기 — shell of one's former self

- 불과하다 — to be nothing

- 겁나다 — to get scared

- 확실하다 — to be sure, to be certain

이해력 문제

1. 만약 병훈이 서둘러 이메일을 점심시간 이전에 발송하고 처리하지 못하면 무슨 일이 일어나나요?
   A) 바로 해고당하고 집으로 돌려보내진다.
   B) 집에 일찍 돌아가 컴퓨터로 비디오 게임을 할 수 있다.
   C) 오년간 승진대상에서 제외된다.
   D) 스케줄이 예정보다 늦어져서 초과근무를 할 가능성이 커진다.

2. 사무실에서 실수가 있으면 징계를 받을 가능성이 있는 사람은 누가 있나요?
   A) 직원
   B) 상사
   C) 직원과 상사
   D) 병훈밖에 없음

3. 인생을 살면서 병훈은 다양한 커리어를 생각해 보았습니다. 해당되지 않는 것은?
   A) 고등학교에서 학생들을 가르치기
   B) 프로게이머가 되기
   C) 프로 수준에서 농구를 하기
   D) 컴퓨터 프로그래머가 되기

4. 동료와 같은 말로는 무엇이 있나요?
   A) 상사
   B) 친구
   C) 감독관
   D) 직장동료

5. 삶의 가혹함에 짓눌린 사람들은 무엇을 겪고 있을 가능성이
   큰 가요?
   A) 복통
   B) 우울증과 불안증
   C) 꿈이 이루어짐
   D) 분위기가 가볍게 됨

English Translation

While Byung-hoon's social life was blooming, his life at work was the polar opposite. He works at an office for an insurance company, and while the pay is good, the workload is overwhelming.

Each morning, he checks his work email to find 50 new requests that have to be immediately dealt with. If he doesn't quickly dispatch and process the emails before lunch, he will get caught behind schedule and most likely have to work overtime. It's extremely stressful and more so when his boss is watching him over his shoulder.

Byung-hoon's boss has to be strict with all the employees. One mistake and it could cost the company a small fortune. Not only will the employee be disciplined harshly, but the boss will be too.

Insurance is a difficult business to work in. It is not for the weak. Meetings, documents, and regulations are all of the utmost importance, and you cannot afford to miss or forget anything. You could be fired for it!

"How am I going to make it to retirement?" Byung-hoon asks himself at least once a week. And he's lucky if this question only comes up once that week. Stress and anxiety are pushing him to his limits. It's only a matter of time before he breaks.

What would life have been like if he had chosen a different college degree? What if he went into computer science? Would he have enjoyed programming more? What if he pushed himself harder while playing for the college baseball team? Would he have made it to the professional level? What if he had made it as a pro-gamer back when he was in school and got to play video games for a living? It would have been a dream come true.

Life didn't turn out that way for Byung-hoon, unfortunately. He might be stuck with a job he hates, but at least he has hope things will change. Many of his co-workers seem to lack that same hope. Depression and anxiety are common in his workplace, but there are a handful of colleagues who are fun to talk to and crack jokes with to lighten the mood. They make it just a little easier to get through each day. That makes all the difference.

There are others, though, who seem to be absolutely crushed by the harshness of life and are now just shells of their former selves. Those people scare Byung-hoon more than any boss ever has.

But when will things change? How will they change? The only thing that is certain is that something must change.

제 5 장

마을과 도시

민서와의 데이트 전, 병훈은 모든걸 미리 준비하기 위해 할 잡다한 일이 몇 개 있었습니다. 먼저, 은행에 들러 바쁜 오늘 하루에 필요한 현금을 인출해야 했습니다. 은행에 가는 길에 병훈은 가장 좋아하는 카페에 들러 힘차게 하루를 시작하기 위해 카페인을 충전합니다.

다음은 우체국에 들러 기한이 만료 되었거나 만료가 임박한 우편물 몇통을 보내야 했습니다. 그 뒤엔 오늘 데이트에 입을 새 옷을 사러 백화점에 가야했습니다. 두 개의 의류점을 둘러본 후 이발소에서 머리를 자를 시간까지 충분했습니다.

오후 2 시에 병훈과 민서는 마을을 둘러볼 준비를 하고 만났습니다. 먼저 공원을 거닐며 주중에 있었던 일들에 대해 서로 이야기를 했습니다. 공원 안에는 커다란 광장이 있었는데, 그들은 그곳에서 작은 락 밴드가 콘서트 하는 것을 발견했습니다. 몇 곡의 노래를 들은 후 그들은 동네 놀이공원으로 향했습니다.

대형 사고로 인해 놀이공원이 문을 닫아야 했기 때문에 대신 영화관을 가기로 결정했습니다. 민서의 운이 좋았는지, 그 주 상영하는 공포영화를 찾을 수 있었습니다. 영화의 시작까지 한 시간을 기다려야 했기 때문에, 가까운 멕시코 식당에서 이른 저녁식사를 하고 시간에 딱 맞춰서 영화관으로 돌아왔습니다. 영화는 꽤 일반적이고 예측 가능했지만 병훈과 민서를 둘 다 정말 깜짝 놀라게 한 장면이 하나 있었습니다.

저녁이 오고 시내에서 너무 늦게까지 있고 싶지 않다고 느꼈고, 스마트폰으로 검색한 특이한 술집에서 술을 한 잔씩 마시기로 동의했습니다. 중세시대의 성 테마를 가지고 있었고, 내부는 휘장, 갑옷, 그리고 왕좌의 모양을 한 의자들로 꾸며져 있었습니다. 두 사람 사이의 대화가 오가면서 술을 더 마시게 되었습니다.

둘 다 시간 가는 줄 모르고 마시다 보니 어느새 밤 11 시였습니다! 곧 지하철이 끊길 예정이었고 아침 6 시까지 다시 운행하지 않기 때문에 집에 돌아갈 시간이 충분하지 않았습니다. 둘은 이제 집에 어떻게 돌아갈지 결정해야 했습니다. 택시를 타고 집에 가기엔 조금 비쌌지만, 아침까지 기다려서 첫차를 타고 돌아가는 것보단 훨씬 나았습니다. 밤새 나이트클럽에서 파티를 하며 시간을 보내고 싶지 않은건 확실했습니다.

하지만 집에 돌아가기 전 조금 더 같이 시간을 보내고 싶었습니다. 그래서 둘은 부두를 따라 걷고 편의점에 들러 간단한 간식을 먹었습니다. 병훈과 민서는 서로 무척 즐거웠지만, 이젠 둘다 심하게 지쳐있는 상태였습니다. 헤어질 시간이 되었습니다. 짧은 입맞춤을 나누고 몇번의 수줍은 미소를 건넨 후, 둘은 따로 택시를 타고 집으로 향했습니다.

단어 목록

- 마을과 도시 — town and city

- 잡다한 일 — errands

- 은행 — bank

- 들르다 — to stop by

- 현금을 인출하다 — to withdraw cash

- 카페 — coffee shop

- 힘차게 — energetically

- 카페인 — caffeine

- 충전하다 — to charge

- 우체국 — post office

- 기한이 만료된 — overdue

- 임박하다 — to be approaching, to be impending

- 우편 — mail

- 옷 — clothes

- 백화점 — mall

- 의류점 — clothing store

- 이발소 — barber shop

- 머리를 자르다 — to get a haircut

- 마을을 둘러보다 — to take a tour around town

- 공원 — park

- 거닐다 — to stroll, to walk
- 주중 — weekday
- 커다란 광장 — large plaza
- 락 밴드 — rock band
- 콘서트 — concert
- 곡 — song
- 동네 — local
- 놀이공원 — amusement park
- 향하다 — to head towards
- 대형 사고 — large accident
- 문을 닫다 — to close down
- 영화관 — movie theater
- 운이 좋다 — to be lucky
- 가까운 — nearby
- 멕시칸 식당 — Mexican restaurant
- 딱 맞추다 — to be just in time
- 꽤 — fairly, pretty
- 일반적인 — generic
- 예측 가능한 — predictable
- 깜짝 놀라다 — to be scared stiff, to be startled
- 장면 — scene

- 저녁 — evening
- 시내 — downtown
- 스마트폰 — smartphone
- 검색하다 — to search the Internet
- 특이한 술집 — a unique bar
- 한 잔씩 — one drink
- 동의하다 — to agree
- 중세시대의 성 — medieval castle
- 테마 — theme
- 내부 — the inside, interior
- 휘장 — banner
- 갑옷 — suit of armor
- 왕좌 — throne
- 모양 — shape, form
- 의자 — chair
- 꾸며지다 — to be decorated
- 시간 가는 줄 모르다 — to lose track of time
- 어느새 — before one knows
- 지하철 — subway
- 끊기다 — to cut off
- 운행하다 — to run (a service e.g. trains and buses)

- 택시를 타다 — to take a taxi
- 첫차 — the first train/bus
- 낫다 — to be better
- 밤새 — all night long
- 나이트클럽 — nightclub
- 파티를 하다 — to party
- 부두 — boardwalk
- 편의점 — convenience store
- 간단한 간식 — a quick snack
- 심하게 지치다 — dead tired
- 상태 — state, condition
- 헤어지다 — to part ways
- 짧은 입맞춤 — brief kiss
- 나누다 — to share
- 수줍은 미소 — cheeky smiles
- 따로 — separate

이해력 문제

1. 은행 계좌에 돈을 넣는걸 뭐라고 하나요?
   A) 출금
   B) 잔액 확인
   C) 계좌 열기
   D) 입금

2. 병훈은 백화점에서 무슨 일을 했나요?
   A) 오락실에서 게임을 했다.
   B) 친구들과 만나 놀고 옷을 구입했다.
   C) 옷을 구입하고 머리를 잘랐다.
   D) 머리를 자르고 푸드코트에서 점심을 먹었다.

3. 병훈과 민서는 공원을 떠나서 어디로 향했나요?
   A) 놀이공원
   B) 집
   C) 영화관
   D) 식당

4. 커플은 중세시대 테마 술집에 대해 어떻게 알게 되었나요?
   A) 술집을 찾아 걸어다녀서.
   B) 서로 알고 있는 친구가 추천해줘서.
   C) 스마트폰으로 가까운 술집을 검색해서.
   D) 술집 광고를 봐서.

5. 시간 가는줄 몰랐단 말은 무엇을 뜻하나요?
   A) 시계를 잃어버렸다.
   B) 시간이 많이 흐른걸 알아채지 못했다.
   C) 시계를 읽는 방법을 잊어버렸다.
   D) 자신의 나이를 잊어버렸다.

English Translation

Before his big date with Min-seo today, Byung-hoon had a few errands to run to make sure everything was ready. First of all, a trip to the bank was needed, so he could withdraw enough cash for the busy day ahead. Along the way to the bank, he stopped by his favorite coffee shop to pick up some much needed caffeine to jump-start the day.

Next, he had to make a run to the post office and drop off some mail that was overdue and nearly late. After that, it was off to the mall to find a new outfit to wear on today's date. He perused two clothing stores and even had enough time to get himself a new haircut at the barber shop.

At 2:00 pm, Byung-hoon and Min-seo met up, ready to take a tour around town. They started by walking around the park, catching up on what happened with each other during the week. Inside the park was a large plaza, where the couple found a small concert by a rock band. After hearing a few songs, they left the park and headed towards a local amusement park.

Due to a large accident, the amusement park had to be shut down, so as a back-up plan, the couple decided to go to the movie theater instead. To Min-seo's luck, they were able to find a horror movie playing that week. It would be an hour-long wait for the movie, so they grabbed an early dinner at a nearby Mexican restaurant with just enough time to make it back to the theater. The movie turned out to be fairly generic and predictable, but there was one jumpscare that got both Byung-hoon and Min-seo really, really good.

As the evening came, the couple had a mutual feeling of not wanting to stay out too late in the city, but they agreed to have one drink at a unique bar they found searching on their smartphones. It had a medieval castle theme and was decorated with banners, suits of armor, and chairs that looked like thrones. The conversation picked up between the two and along with it came more drinking.

They both lost track of time and before they knew it it was 11:00 pm! The subway was closing soon, and they would not have enough time to make it back home. It would not open until 6:00 AM, so they now had to decide how they would return home. Taking a taxi home would be a bit expensive, but it was much better than waiting until morning for the early train. They definitely did not want to spend that time at nightclubs partying all night.

Before going home however, the couple did want to spend a little more time together, so they walked along the boardwalk and stopped by the convenience store for a quick snack. Byung-hoon and Min-seo thoroughly enjoyed each other's presence, but they were now both dead tired. It was time to part ways. A brief kiss was shared, along with a couple of cheeky smiles, and that was it before they both took separate taxis and headed home.

제 6 장

집에서 쉬는날

때는 일요일 오후, 병훈은 별다른 계획이 없어 일주일간 밀렸던 잠을 따라잡기 위해 늦잠을 잤습니다. 완전히 게으름만 피우는 날은 아닙니다. 해야할 집안일이 몇가지 있기 때문입니다.

가장 중요한 일은 아마 미납 청구서들을 처리하는 것 일겁니다. 빌린 방에 사는건 공짜가 아니니까요. 집세, 전기세, 수도세, 인터넷비, 학자금, 그리고 핸드폰 요금까지 모두 납부 기한이 있습니다. 다행히 기술의 발전 덕분에 집을 나서지 않고도 집에서 모두 온라인으로 납부할 수 있습니다.

그 다음은 일주일간 쌓여온 빨래를 하는 일입니다. 다가오는 한 주를 위해선 빨래를 여러 번 해야 할 것입니다. 한번도 빨래를 흰 색, 어두운 색, 그리고 밝은 색으로 나눈적이 없습니다. 대신, 그저 통에 들어가는 만큼 최대한 많은 양을 던져넣고 세제와 섬유유연제를 조금 따라넣은 후 세탁기를 돌릴 뿐이었죠.

빨래 한 짐이 돌아가는 동안 그는 설거지를 하고 청소기를 돌리면서 생산적인 시간을 보내기로 합니다. 병훈의 아파트는 티끌 하나 없이 깨끗하진 않지만 매주 할 수 있는만큼 조금씩 청소했습니다. 이번주는 부엌일을 조금 더 하기로 했습니다. 냉장고를 청소하며 유통기한이 지난 음식을 버리고, 부엌 식탁을 소독제로 닦고, 바닥에서 음식 부스러기를 쓸어냈습니다. 끝으로 바닥을 빗자루와 쓰레받이로 쓸었습니다. 걸레질은 다음주에 해도 되겠다고 그는 생각했습니다.

병훈은 하루의 남은 시간을 컴퓨터로 게임을 하며 보내는데 더 관심이 많았습니다. 그는 전략 게임을 좋아해서 온라인에서 친구들을 같이 하거나 심지어 싱글 플레이어 게임을 할때에도 새로운 전략을 고안하는데 몇 시간이고 보낼 수 있었습니다. 휴식이 필요할때면 가끔씩 일어나 간단한 스트레칭을 하고, 창 밖을 내다보고, 전자레인지로 음식을 데우고, 다시 게임을 하러 앉곤 했습니다.

컴퓨터 앞에서 너무 많은 시간을 보낸 후에는 존재론적 위기 상황이 오곤 합니다. 다른 의미있는 일을 하지 않고 그 많은 시간을 게임에 보낸게 과연 현명한 일이었을까요? 물론 온라인으로 시청할 수 있는 영상이 많긴 했지만, 그런다고 무엇이 달라질까요? 그래서 그는 침실에 있는 헤드폰을 쓰고 민서가 추천해준 오디오북을 듣기 시작했습니다.

오디오책을 듣기 시작하니 곧장 시간을 올바르게 쓰는 것 같은 기분이 들었고 자기 성찰의 기회도 열렸습니다. 계속 들으면서 그는 아파트 내를 거닐었습니다. 아무 이유없이 옷장문을 열었다 닫고, 소파에 손을 얹고 걸어 지나가며 미끄러져 내림을 반복했습니다. 그는 혼자 살아서 주로 부엌이나 베란다에서 식사를 했기 때문에, 거실에서는 이런 짓을 다시 할 식탁이 없었습니다.

어느새 오후 10시가 되어서 침대로 향할 시간이었습니다. 오디오북을 끝내진 못했지만 다음 주말 가족 모임에 가면 할 새로운 이야기가 생긴 것은 분명했습니다. 자신에게 책을 추천한 사람으로서 민서를 데려가 소개할 수도 있을 것 입니다.

단어 목록

- 집에서 쉬는 날 — taking the day off at home

- 일요일 오후 — Sunday afternoon

- 별다른 계획 — particular plans

- 밀리다 — to be overdue

- 따라잡다 — to catch up

- 늦잠을 자다 — to sleep in

- 게으름을 피우다 — to be lazy

- 집안일 — household chores

- 미납 청구서 — unpaid bills

- 빌린 방 — a rented room

- 공짜 — free

- 집세 — rent

- 전기세 — electricity bill

- 수도세 — water bill

- 인터넷 — internet

- 학자금 — student loans

- 핸드폰 요금 — phone bill

- 납부 기한이 있다 — to have a payment due

- 다행히 — fortunately

- 기술 — technology

- 집을 나서다 — to leave home
- 온라인으로 납부하다 — to pay online
- 빨래 — laundry
- 흰 색 — white
- 어두운 색 — dark colors
- 밝은 색 — bright colors
- 나누다 — to sort
- 던져넣다 — to throw in
- 세제 — laundry detergent
- 섬유유연제 — fabric softener
- 따라넣다 — to pour in
- 세탁기 — laundry machine
- 기계를 돌리다 — to run a machine
- 빨래 한 짐 — a load of laundry
- 설거지를 하다 — to do the dishes
- 청소기를 돌리다 — to vacuum
- 생산적인 — productive
- 티끌 하나 없이 깨끗하다 — spotless
- 부엌 — kitchen
- 냉장고를 청소하다 — to clean out the fridge
- 유통기한이 지난 음식 — expired food

- 버리다 — to throw away

- 부엌 식탁 — kitchen table

- 소독제 — disinfectant

- 닦다 — to scrub

- 바닥 — floor

- 음식 부스러기 — food crumbs

- 쓸어내다 — to sweep away

- 빗자루와 쓰레받이 — broom and dustpan

- 쓸다 — to sweep

- 걸레질 — mopping

- 하루의 남은 시간 — the rest of the day

- 전략 게임 — strategy games

- 싱글 플레이어 게임 — single player games

- 휴식 — break, rest

- 창 밖을 내다보다 — to peer out the windows

- 전자레인지 — microwave

- 데우다 — to heat up

- 존재론적 위기 상황 — existential crisis

- 의미있는 — meaningful

- 현명한 — wise

- 온라인으로 시청하다 — to watch online

- 영상 — videos
- 침실 — bedroom
- 헤드폰을 쓰다 — to put on headphones
- 추천하다 — to recommend
- 곧장 — right away
- 올바르게 — rightly
- 자기 성찰 — self-reflection
- 기회가 열리다 — to open up the opportunity
- 아무 이유없이 — for no particular reason
- 옷장 문 — closet doors
- 소파 — couch
- 걸어 지나가다 — to walk by
- 미끄러져 내리다 — to glide over
- 반복하다 — to repeat
- 혼자 살다 — to live by oneself
- 베란다 — porch, veranda
- 거실 — living room
- 짓 — act
- 침대로 향할 시간 — time for bed
- 가족 모임 — family gathering
- 소개하다 — to introduce

이해력 문제

1. 밀린 잠을 따라잡는 것은 무엇을 의미하는 말인가요?
    A) 너무 많이 잤다
    B) 너무 조금 잤다
    C) 자는 것을 좋아한다
    D) 잠드는데 어려움이 있다

2. 다음 중 집과 관련된 납부금이 아닌 것은?
    A) 학자금
    B) 수도세
    C) 전기세
    D) 인터넷비

3. 병훈이 부엌을 청소하면서 하지 않은 것은?
    A) 소독제로 부엌 식탁을 청소하기
    B) 유통기한이 지난 음식 버리기
    C) 바닥을 걸레질하기
    D) 빗자루와 쓰레받이로 바닥을 쓸기

4. 다음중 일반적으로 가장 빨리 요리를 할 수 있는 도구는 무엇인가요?
    A) 스토브
    B) 전자레인지
    C) 오븐
    D) 토스터 오븐

5. 병훈은 어디서 헤드폰을 찾았나요?
    A) 그의 침실에서
    B) 그의 옷장에서
    C) 그의 세탁기에서
    D) 그의 거실에서

English Translation

It was a Sunday afternoon. Byung-hoon had no particular plans, so he slept in and allowed himself to catch up on sleep he had missed during the week. It would not be a completely lazy day though, for he had a number of household chores to do.

Perhaps most important of all were the unpaid bills that needed to be taken care of. Housing isn't free, after all. Rent, electricity, water, internet, student loans, and phone plans all have payments due. Thanks to technology, however, all of these can be paid online without leaving the house.

Next, the laundry had piled up over the week, and a few loads would be necessary for the upcoming week. He never bothered to sort his laundry into whites, darks, and colors; instead, he would just throw as much as he could in each load, pour in some laundry detergent and fabric softener, and run the laundry machine.

While he waited for each load to finish, he figured he would stay productive by doing the dishes and vacuuming the apartment. Byung-hoon's apartment was by no means spotless, but he did just a little bit each week to maintain what he could. This week, he would do some extra work in the kitchen. He cleaned out the fridge by throwing away expired foods. He also scrubbed the counters with disinfectant and brushed off all food crumbs to the floor. And he finished by sweeping the floor with his broom and dustpan. Mopping could wait another week, he thought.

Byung-hoon was more interested in spending the rest of his day at the computer playing video games. He was a fan of strategy games and could spend hours coming up with new strategies to try out against his friends online and even in single player games. When he needed a break, he would occasionally get up for a quick stretch, peer out the windows, heat up some food in the microwave, and sit back down for more gaming.

After spending too many hours in front of the computer, a small existential crisis would occur. Was it really all that wise to spend so much time gaming when it could be used for something more meaningful? Sure, there were videos he could watch online, but would that be any different? And so, he picked up the headphones in his bedroom and started to listen to some of the audiobook recommended to him by Min-seo.

Listening to the book instantly felt like the right use of his time and even opened up the opportunity for some self-reflection. As he kept listening, he wandered around his apartment. He opened and closed his closet doors for no particular reason. He put his hand on the couch and let it glide over as he walked across. There was no dining room table to repeat this action, as he lived by himself and usually ate in the kitchen or out on the balcony.

Before he knew it, it was 10:00 pm. It was time for bed. While he didn't finish the audiobook, he certainly had something new to talk about next weekend when he would go to the family gathering. He could even bring Min-seo and introduce her as the one who introduced him to the book.

제 7 장

가족과 직업

민서는 다음 주말 병훈의 가족 모임에 함께하는 것에 흔쾌히 응했습니다. 이제 공식적으로 커플이였기 때문에 그의 어머니, 아버지, 그리고 형제들에게 소개하기 좋은 시간이라고 생각했기 때문입니다.

또한 모임에는 병훈의 삼촌인 정철도 참석했습니다. 정철은 기계 공학자로서 증기와 가스 터빈과 전기 발전기를 포함한 다양한 기계를 다루는 분이었습니다. 그는 아주 총명한 사람이었고, 병훈의 어린시절에 많은 도움이 되었습니다.

그의 삼촌과 대화하던 도중, 병훈은 그의 사촌들인 시우와 수아가 뒤에 있는 것을 알아차렸습니다. 셋은 어릴적 함께 어울려 놀던 사이였고 많은 어린시절 추억을 함께 나눈 사이였습니다. 나이가 들면서 안타깝게도 사이가 서먹해졌고, 직장 생활을 시작하면서 서로 연락이 끊어진 상태였습니다. 시우는 한 소매점의 관리직으로 나아가는 중이였고 수아는 파트타임 미용사이자 풀타임 엄마가 되었습니다.

당연하게도, 처음 보는 얼굴들 사이에서 민서는 긴장됐지만, 행사에서 알아가게 된 사람이 한 명 있었습니다. 바로 병훈의 형수인 지아였습니다. 처음부터 두 사람은 죽이 잘 맞았고 바로 친밀한 사이가 되었습니다. 민서는 기자였고, 지아는 같은 언론 회사에서 제작하는 티비 프로그램의 작가였습니다. 미무실에서 몇번 본적은 있지만 이렇게 만난 것은 이번이 처음이였습니다.

　민서가 전부 만나기엔 너무나 많은 사람들이 있었습니다. 심지어 병훈에게도 모두와 안부인사를 하기에 충분하지 않은 시간이었습니다. 그의 할머니와 이모들에게 간단히 인사를 했지만 조카들과 이야기 할 시간은 전혀 없었습니다. 모든 아이들은 다른 방에서 함께 노느라 바빴습니다.

　가족 단체사진을 찍었는데, 민서 또한 함께 찍도록 권유 받았습니다. 매년, 병훈의 아버지는 최고의 가족사진을 만드는 임무를 맡습니다. 전문 사진작가이기 때문에 그에게 이 일을 맡기는건 당연한 일이었습니다.

　해가 지기 시작했고 시간이 늦어지고 있었습니다. 사람들이 모두 떠날때 쯤, 병훈은 그의 삼촌인 정철과 다시 한번 이야기할 기회가 있었습니다. 그는 현재 보험회사에서 근무하면서 지쳐가고 있는 걱정에 대해 얘기하고, 갈 수 있는 여러 길을 생각 중이라고 말했습니다. 정철 삼촌은 앞으로 어디서 일하고 싶은지 확실하지 않더라도 가능한 빨리 수업을 듣기 시작해야 한다고 조언했습니다. 시작하기만을 기다리는건 그가 할 수 있는 최악의 일이였기 때문입니다.

단어 목록

- 가족과 직업 — family and occupations
- 함께 하다 — to join, to be with
- 흔쾌히 — willingly, gladly
- 응하다 — to accept
- 공식적으로 — officially
- 커플 — couple
- 어머니 — mother
- 아버지 — father
- 형제들 — brothers
- ~하기 좋은 시간이다 — to be a good time to
- 삼촌 — uncle
- 참석하다 — to attend
- 기계 공학자 — mechanical engineer
- 증기와 가스 터빈 — steam and gas turbines
- 전기 발전기 — electric generators
- 다루다 — to handle, to deal with
- 아주 총명한 — extremely intelligent
- 어린시절 — childhood
- 사촌 — cousin
- 알아차리다 — to realize

- 어울려 놀다 — to hang out

- 추억 — memories

- 나이가 들다 — to get older

- 서먹하다 — to feel awkward

- 연락이 끊어지다 — to lose contact

- 소매점 — retail store

- 관리직 — management position

- 파트타임 — part-time

- 미용사 — hairdresser

- 풀타임 — full-time

- 엄마 — mom

- 당연하게도 — obviously

- 행사 — event

- 바로 — precisely

- 형수 — sister-in-law

- 처음부터 — from the beginning

- 죽이 잘 맞다 — to hit it off

- 친밀한 사이가 되다 — to establish rapport

- 기자 — journalist

- 언론 회사 — media company

- 제작하다 — to produce

- 티비 프로그램 — TV show

- 작가 — writer

- 안부인사하다 — to say hello, to greet

- 할머니 — grandmother

- 이모 — aunts

- 조카 — nieces/nephews

- 단체사진 — group photo

- 권유 받다 — to be invited

- 임무를 맡다 — to take on a task

- 전문 — professional, expert

- 사진작가 — photographer

- 해가 지다 — the sun sets

- 가능한 빨리 — as soon as possible

- 수업을 듣다 — to take classes

- 조언하다 — to advise

- 최악 — the worst

이해력 문제

1. 병훈의 삼촌의 직업은 무엇인가요?
    A) 전기 공학자
    B) 토목 공학자
    C) 화학 공학자
    D) 기계 공학자

2. 시우와 수아의 부모님은 병훈에게 무슨 관계인가요?
    A) 할아버지와 할머니
    B) 어머니와 아버지
    C) 이모와 이모부
    D) 남동생과 여동생

3. 병훈의 형수는 누구와 결혼했나요?
    A) 그의 형
    B) 그의 아버지
    C) 그의 사촌
    D) 그의 상사

4. 가족 모임동안 아이들은 어디서 놀고 있었나요?
    A) 학교에서
    B) 지하실에서
    C) 다른 방에서
    D) 장난감 가게에서

5. 어떤 직업에 대해 높은 자격을 갖춘 사람들 뭐라고 부르나요?
    A) 아마추어
    B) 직장 생활
    C) 직업
    D) 전문가

English Translation

Min-seo happily agreed to accompany Byung-hoon on his visit to his family gathering the following weekend. They were now officially a couple, and it would be a good time to introduce her to his mother, father, and brothers.

Also at the get-together was Byung-hoon's uncle, named Jong-chul. Jong-chul was a mechanical engineer, who worked on all kinds of machines, including steam and gas turbines and electric generators. He was an extremely intelligent man, who helped guide Byung-hoon in his younger years.

While chatting with his uncle, he noticed his two cousins Si-hoo and Soo-ah in the background. The three of them hung out quite frequently as kids and shared a lot of childhood memories. They grew apart as they got older, unfortunately, and lost contact with one another as they entered the workforce. Si-hoo ended up working his way up to a management position at a retail store. And Soo-ah was a part-time hairdresser but a full-time mom.

Min-seo was obviously overwhelmed by all the new faces, but she was able to get to know at least one person at the event. This person was Byung-hoon's sister-in-law Ji-ah. From the very get-go, the two hit it off and established an instant rapport. Min-seo was a journalist by trade, and Ji-ah was a writer for a TV show that was produced by the same media company they both worked for. While they had seen each other around the office, they had never met until now.

In the end, there were just too many people for Min-seo to meet and even for Byung-hoon to catch up with. They briefly said hello to his grandmother and aunts, but they never got the chance to greet his nieces and nephews. All the kids were busy playing together in a separate room.

The family was able to take a group photo, which included Min-seo, who was invited to join in. Every year, it's Byung-hoon's dad who is given the task to create the best family photo possible. Leaving the task to him makes sense, given that he's a professional photographer.

The sun started going down, and the day was growing late. As everyone was leaving, Byung-hoon had another opportunity to speak with his Uncle Jong-chul. He voiced his concerns about burning out at his current job at the insurance company and was considering a few possible paths he could take. Uncle Jong-chul advised him that, even though he's not sure where he wants to work in the future, he should definitely start taking classes as soon as possible. Waiting to start was the worst thing he could possibly do.

제 8 장

교육

풀타임 직업에 여자친구까지 둔 병훈의 스케줄은 상당히 빡빡했습니다. 하지만 더 나은 미래를 위해 가까운 대학교에서 경제학 대학원 과정에 등록했습니다. 병훈은 이미 학부생 과정을 졸업하고 철학과 학사 학위를 취득했지만, 많은 문과 학위가 그렇듯 직장을 구하거나 새로운 커리어를 시작하는데 있어서는 최선의 선택이 아니었습니다.

이번에는 다를 것입니다. 더 많은 경험과 지혜로 더욱 많은 교육을 받을 수 있는 이 기회를 헛되이 하지 않을 것입니다. 경제학 대학원 과정은 만만치 않은 도전이 될테지만, 성공한다면 그 보상은 아주 값질 것입니다. 이것에 비교하면 학부생 시절 들었던 수업들은 식은죽 먹기일 것입니다. 철저하게 공부해야 하고 끈기도 필요할 것입니다.

교과서가 종종 강의보다 훨씬 더 유용했습니다. 어떤 교수님들은 너무 장황한 설명을 해서 수업시간에 집중을 하기가 어려웠습니다. 강의의 절반도 안되는 시간동안 교과서를 읽으면, 강의실에서 배운 지식의 두 배를 얻을 수 있을 정도 였습니다. 반면에 조교들은 복잡한 개념도 간단한 용어를 사용해 설명할 수 있었기 때문에 가장 많은 도움이 되었습니다.

배운 정보를 확실히 입력시키기 위해선 교실 밖에서의 더 많은 노력이 필요했습니다. 학생들이 조직한 스터디그룹은 병훈이 과정을 성공적으로 수료하기 위해 필요한 동기부여와 추진력을 제공하는데 중요한 역할을 했습니다. 모임 내에서 학생들은 수업중 적은 필기를 비교하고 시험에 나올 것으로 예상되는 정보들을 검토했습니다. 항상 진지하기만 했던건 아닙니다. 가끔씩 쌓인 스트레스와 불만감을 해소하기 위해 수다 떠는 휴식 시간이 자주 있었기 때문입니다.

첫 해의 기말고사가 다가오고 있었고 마지막 몇 번의 강의 동안에는 교실에 불안감이 가득했습니다. 시험에는 객관식이 아닌 논술형 문제만 있을 예정이라 벼락치기는 이번 시험에 아무런 도움도 되지 않을 것입니다. 좋은 학점을 받으려면 내용을 확실히 이해해야 했습니다. 병훈과 그의 반 친구들은 모두 비싼 등록금을 냈지만 모두가 시험에 합격하진 못할겁니다. 수업에 참석하고, 스터디그룹에 참여하고, 꼼꼼하게 읽은 사람들만이 높은 점수로 합격할 수 있을 것입니다.

그것은 외국어를 배우는 것과 아주 흡사했습니다. 외국어 습득을 가장 잘 하는 사람들은 외국어에 완전히 몰입하는 사람들입니다. 그들은 배우고 싶은 언어로 된 글을 최대한 많이 읽고, 읽을 거리가 더이상 없으면 남은 자유시간을 전부 그 언어를 듣는 연습을 하는데 씁니다. 오랜 취미나 생활 방식보다 이러한 언어 몰입하는 것을 우선시합니다. 그렇게 해서 그들이 그 정도로 유창해 질 수 있는 것입니다.

진짜 중요한 문제는 병훈의 기말고사 합격여부가 아닌, 여러분이 언어에 유창해지기 위해 필요한 모든 일을 할 것이냐에 달려있습니다.

즐거운 공부 되세요! 그리고 지금까지 읽어주셔서 감사합니다!

단어 목록

- 교육 — education
- 여자친구 — girlfriend
- 상당히 — quite, rather
- 빡빡하다 — tight, intensive
- 대학교 — university
- 경제학 — economics
- 대학원 과정 — graduate program
- 등록하다 — to enroll
- 학부생 과정 — undergraduate program
- 졸업하다 — to graduate
- 철학 — philosophy
- 학사 학위 — bachelor's degree
- 취득하다 — to acquire
- 문과 학위 — liberal arts degrees
- 직장을 구하다 — to seek employment
- 커리어를 시작하다 — to start a career
- 최선 — the best way
- 경험 — experience
- 지혜 — wisdom
- 더욱 많은 교육을 받다 — to further one's education

- 헛되다 — to be vain

- 만만치 않은 도전 — formidable challenge

- 보상 — reward

- 값지다 — to be valuable

- 비교하다 — to compare

- 식은죽 먹기 — cakewalk (literally "eating cold porridge")

- 철저한 공부 — intense study

- 끈기 — perseverance

- 교과서 — textbooks

- 종종 — often

- 강의 — lectures

- 유용하다 — to be useful

- 교수님 — professor

- 장황한 설명 — a long-winded explanation

- 집중을 유지하다 — to maintain focus

- 절반 — half

- 강의실 — lecture hall

- 지식 — knowledge

- 두 배 — double

- 반면에 — on the other hand

- 조교 — teaching assistant

- 복잡한 개념 — complex concepts
- 간단한 용어 — basic language
- 정보를 확실히 입력시키다 — to make information stick
- 교실 — classroom
- 학생 — students
- 조직하다 — to organize
- 스터디 그룹 — study group
- 과정 — course
- 수료하다 — to complete
- 동기부여 — motivation
- 추진력 — momentum
- 제공하다 — to provide
- 역할하다 — to play a role
- 필기 — notes
- 시험 — exam
- 예상되다 — to be expected
- 검토하다 — to review information
- 진지하다 — to be serious
- 쌓인 — built-up
- 불만감 — frustration
- 해소하다 — to vent

- 수다 떨다 — to chit-chat

- 첫 해 — first year

- 기말고사 — finals

- 객관식 — multiple choice

- 논술형 문제 — essay questions

- 벼락치기 — cramming

- 좋은 학점 — good grade

- 내용 — content

- 반 친구 — classmate

- 등록금 — tuition fees

- 시험에 합격하다 — to pass the test

- 참여하다 — to participate

- 꼼꼼하게 읽다 — to read extensively

- 높은 점수 — high marks

- 외국어 — foreign language

- 흡사하다 — to resemble

- 습득하다 — to acquire

- 몰입하다 — to be immersed

- 언어 — language

- 자유시간 — free time

- 오랜 취미 — old hobby

- 생활 방식 — lifestyle

- 우선시하다 — to take precedence

- 유창하다 — to be fluent

- 합격 여부 — success or failure

- 달려있다 — to depend on

이해력 문제

1. 병훈은 어디서 경제학 강의를 듣고 있나요?
   A) 온라인 프로그램을 통해
   B) 지역 대학교에서
   C) 전문 학교에서
   D) 과외를 통해서

2. 만만치 않은 도전이라고 말할 때 무엇을 뜻하나요?
   A) 쉽다
   B) 불가능하다
   C) 위협적이다
   D) 가능하다

3. 강의의 가장 큰 문제는 무엇이었나요?
   A) 수업이 밤에 진행 되었다.
   B) 병훈의 친구들이 수업 도중 계속 말을 했다.
   C) 교수님의 설명이 너무 복잡했다.
   D) 교수님이 학생들을 싫어했다.

4. 스터디 그룹을 조직한건 누구인가요?
   A) 학생들
   B) 조교들
   C) 병훈
   D) 교수님

5. 기말고사는 어떤 형식의 시험이었나요?
   A) 전부 객관식
   B) 객관식과 논술형 문제의 조합
   C) 벼락치기와 비싼 등록금의 조합
   D) 전부 논술형

English Translation

With a full-time job and a girlfriend, Byung-hoon's schedule was pretty tightly packed. But for the sake of a better future, he enrolled in a graduate program for economics at his local university. Byung-hoon had already completed an undergraduate program and graduated with a bachelor's degree in philosophy, yet like most liberal arts degrees, it was not the greatest choice for seeking employment and starting a career.

This time would be different. With much more experience and wisdom, this opportunity to further his education would not go wasted. A graduate program in economics was going to be a formidable challenge, but if he succeeded, the rewards would be great. The classes he took as an undergraduate would be a cakewalk compared to this. Intense study and perseverance would be required.

The textbooks would often prove to be much more useful than the lectures. Some of the professors he had talked with such long-winded delivery that it was incredibly difficult to maintain focus in class. He could spend half the time reading chapters from the book and come away with double the information he got in the lecture hall. The teacher assistants, however, were most helpful, as they could explain complex concepts using very basic language.

To make the information stick, serious work was needed to be done outside the classroom. Study groups organized by students were instrumental in providing Byung-hoon the motivation and drive required to do well in the course. In the groups, students shared the notes they took in class and reviewed the information they thought would appear on the exams. Not all this time was serious though, as there were multiple breaks where chit-chat was encouraged as a means to vent built-up stress and frustration.

Finals for the first year were approaching, and anxiety filled the classroom during the last few lectures. On the test would be essay questions only; there would be no multiple choice. Cramming wasn't going to get you anywhere on this test. You had to know the information in order to get a good grade. Byung-hoon and all his classmates paid hefty tuition fees, but not all would pass the test. It would be those who attended the lectures, participated in the study groups, and read extensively that would pass with high marks.

It was very much like learning a foreign language. Those who do the best are those who immerse themselves in the foreign language. They read as much as possible in the target language, and when they can no longer read, they spend all their free time listening to the target language. Immersion takes precedence over their old hobbies and lifestyles. That's how they achieve high levels of fluency.

The question is not whether or not Byung-hoon passed the final exam. The true question is whether or not you will do what it takes in order to achieve fluency.

Happy studying! And thank you for reading!

DID YOU ENJOY THE READ?

Thank you so much for taking the time to read our book! We hope you have enjoyed it and learned tons of vocabulary in the process.

If you would like to support our work, please consider writing a customer review on Amazon, Goodreads, or wherever you purchased our book from. It would mean the world to us!

We read each and every single review posted, and we use all the feedback we receive to write even better books.

ANSWER KEY

Chapter 1:
1) C
2) D
3) B
4) C
5) C

Chapter 2:
1) B
2) C
3) A
4) D
5) B

Chapter 3:
1) D
2) B
3) A
4) C
5) C

Chapter 4:
1) D
2) C
3) A
4) D

Chapter 5:
1) D
2) C
3) A
4) C
5) B

Chapter 6:
1) B
2) A
3) C
4) B
5) A

Chapter 7:
1) D
2) C
3) A
4) C
5) D

Chapter 8:
1) B
2) C
3) C
4) A

Made in the USA
Middletown, DE
25 September 2023

39362060R00050